RYAN NEWELL

Manipulation Psychology

The Easy Guide For The World of Manipulation Psychology, To Defense Yourself Against Manipulator and Mind Control

Copyright © 2021 Ryan Newell

All rights reserved.

© **Copyright 2021 - All rights reserved.**

The content contained within this book may not be reproduced, duplicated or transmitted without direct written permission from the author or the publisher.

Under no circumstances will any blame or legal responsibility be held against the publisher, or author, for any damages, reparation, or monetary loss due to the information contained within this book. Either directly or indirectly.

Legal Notice:

This book is copyright protected. This book is only for personal use. You cannot amend, distribute, sell, use, quote or paraphrase any part, or the content within this book, without the consent of the author or publisher.

Disclaimer Notice:

Please note the information contained within this document is for educational and entertainment purposes only. All effort has been executed to present accurate, up to date, and reliable, complete information. No warranties of any kind are declared or implied. Readers acknowledge that the author is not engaging in the rendering of legal, financial, medical or professional advice. The content within this book has been derived from various sources. Please consult a licensed professional before attempting any techniques outlined in this book.

By reading this document, the reader agrees that under no circumstances is the author responsible for any losses, direct or indirect, which are incurred as a result of the use of information contained within this document, including, but not limited to, — errors, omissions, or inaccuracies.

Table of Content

Introduction 4

Chapter 1. Reading People Through Their Mind 10

Chapter 2. Myths About Body Language 18

Chapter 3. Who Is a Manipulator? 25

Chapter 4. Dark Psychology and Women 32

Chapter 5. Techniques of Dark Psychology 39

Chapter 6. Practical Exercises For Mind Control Prevention 46

Chapter 7. Touch As a Form of Body Language 52

Chapter 8. Facial Expression As a Form of Body 57

Conclusion 65

Introduction

First of all, we must dialog about why it is different from reading a child's body language. The first reason is that they are young and have not yet learned to control their emotions. If a child is sad, they cry. If a child is happy, they smile. If they are angry, they yell and make mad faces, and if they are embarrassed, their cheeks turn red, and they hide their face. Some children might even decide to tell you about the emotions that they are feeling. Children are new to the world and have no reason to hide the things they are going through.

Because of this, children have body language that is extremely easy to read. They do not distinguish how to control their emotions, so they always show how they feel. If you read the emotions of a child, you are reading what they truly feel.

Another important thing to note about reading the body language of children is that since they do not yet know how to hide their emotions, they also are unaware of the body language signs that they portray. They are not capable of sending the opposite signal of how they feel like adults are.

Their lack of awareness of their own body language can also make it easy to spot when a child is lying. A child might try to hide the truth through their words, but they do not have the wherewithal to think to conceal it in their body language as well, often allowing tells to slip through that they are not telling the truth or are omitting part of the truth.

For example, my sister has a five-year-old daughter who likes to sneak chocolate chip cookies before dinner. My sister always checks the Chips Ahoy package right before she starts making dinner, so she knows when a cookie is missing. She will still ask her daughter in the hopes that her daughter will confess on her own. My niece will most of the time try to lie about it (my personal favorite being when she claimed her father ate the cookie). However, no matter how convincing she might think she sounds, she has one big tell that she is lying: a huge smile plastered on her face. Because she thinks she is getting away with something so mischievous, this smile appears on her face as she is so proud of her deceit. When it is clear that she will not get away with it, this smile is usually replaced by another tell, i.e., her hanging her head while looking at the floor because she is ashamed at having been caught.

Everyone has the physical tell that gives them away when they are lying. Fortunately for parents, guardians, and teachers, children are unable to hide their tells until they are older and have more experience both with lying and reading their own body language.

Today that we know how simple it is to read the body language of a child, let's look into how important it is to pay attention to the signals a child is conveying. Whether you are around children a lot or not, you need to be able to read a child's body language so that you can do your part in ensuring that our children are healthy and safe. Like reading an adult's body language can help us determine if they are in a dangerous situation, we can also use a child's body language to determine if they are in any danger. The unlucky truth is that we live in a world in which people will abuse, kidnap, and otherwise harm children. We want to help children out of such situations, but it can often be hard to tell when something suspicious is going on.

Reading a child's body language can help us determine if there is more to the state than meets the eye. Because young children do not know how to control their body language, any discomfort they feel around a specific adult will manifest in such ways as to how they hold themselves around this person. For instance, if a child exhibits such body language as standing stiffly, hunching their shoulders forward to make themselves smaller, or avoiding eye contact with everyone, including the adult they are with, it could mean that they are afraid of something. If they flinch whenever the adult that they are with reaches over to touch them, it could very well mean that this fear stems from someone hurting them on a regular basis, most likely this adult. Also, suppose they refuse to initiate physical contact with this adult while still never wandering any significant distance from them. In that case, it could mean that they are afraid to have any intimacy with this adult and of doing anything to anger them.

Mind you, none of this is a reason to call the police or Child Protective Services on someone. After all, there are multiple interpretations of any given body language. Standing stiffly, hunching their shoulders forward, or avoiding eye contact, for example, could just mean that the child is not comfortable in that particular environment or with strangers. Flinching and avoiding initiating physical contact with the adult could indicate, rather than fear, that the child has a problem with physical touch overall or that they are mad with that adult for some reason. Not wandering far from the adult, even though it is natural for a child to want to explore, could simply show that the child is well behaved or not particularly comfortable with checking out their surroundings on their own.

Like with all body language reading, what a child's body language means often depends on the context. If you know the child and adult personally, it can be easier to determine what the child's body language means. If they are complete strangers, it will be trickier. Nevertheless, spotting such body language in a child will help you to be on alert so that if suspicion arises that the child is being abused or has been kidnapped, you will be ready to take action.

Reading a child's body language will also help you to be there for them emotionally. If you have a child or take care of a child for large amounts of time, they will consider you their support system. They need you to help them learn about their lives and the world around them. It includes learning how to handle their emotions.

Sometimes, a child might have an emotion that they do not yet know how to explain. They may express this feeling through body language but still feel frustrated when they are unable to put their experience into words.

As an adult who distinguishes how to read body language, you can help in this situation. You can read the nonverbal cues that the child is portraying and use them to help the child express his or her feelings verbally. It will help the child learn about their feelings and more about who they are. It will also help the child grow up knowing that feelings are healthy and that it is okay to share your struggles with those close to you. If you can help your child in this way and teach these things to your child at a young age, they will have significantly fewer emotional struggles over the course of their life. This understanding is important to any adult who deals with children, such as doctors, teachers, and parents dealing with other kids, such as their children's friends.

Parents and caregivers need to teach their children how to express their own body language. Still, they need to teach the kids about simple body language reading techniques. You might not want to call it body language reading to them because they either will not understand or will think the topic is boring, but this skill must be taught to children in whatever creative way necessary.

You might wonder why I believe it is important for children to be able to read body language since it is a science-based topic that can be complicated at times. We will explain why this is important now.

First, if your children understand that nonverbal communication has just as much meaning as the words they speak, they will understand the people around them at a new level. Take their time on the playground, for example. If they ask a friend to play with them and the friend says no but is looking at the ground and has another child staring at them as if to tell them not to play with the child, they will know that there is more meaning behind this situation. They will either be able to speak up for their friend and encourage them to do what they want. Or they will be deprived of worrying about what other people think or be able to walk away without feeling offended because they know that there was more to the conversation than a simple denied request to play. It might even be a sign that the friend was bullied away from playing, and your child will be able to express to a trusted adult what they saw.

Also, think about if your child sees a classmate that is not saying much when they usually talk all day, every day. If your child is aware of the body language of the people around them, they might notice this difference in behavior and ask the child what is wrong. It could make a profound change in the said child's day.

You might even consider the friendships that the child already has. As an adult, you know that being able to read simple body language allows you to have better friendships. It makes sense, then, that the same is true with friendships among children.

Your child will also be able to avoid being a bully better if they are aware of their own body language. They will understand that actions like rolling the eyes or walking away from someone when they are talking to them hurt just as much as mean words. They will understand these actions and avoid them to be nice to the people around them when other children might accidentally hurt their friends with actions like these without knowing the consequences.

When a child knows body language, they are able to make sure that their friends are comfortable with them. If the child sits close to a friend, they will be able to tell if the friend is okay with close contact or not. If the friend is not tolerable and shows signs of being uncomfortable, the child will know that the right thing is to move away.

A lot of these types of body language are things that children learn through real-life experience. The only problem with this is that real feelings are getting hurt if they are learning in real life, and real friends are feeling uncomfortable. The sooner a child acquires these skills, the sooner they can use body language to their advantage.

Chapter 1. Reading People Through Their Mind

How often have you heard somebody instruct you to simply say something because they can't guess what you might be thinking?

Things being what they are, this is just half evident. The individual disclosing to you this may not know, yet they are positively equipped to guess what you might be thinking. They do what desires to be done in a more unpretentious way than they see.

A great many people can actually figure out how to guess thoughts with preparing, time, center, and a specific arrangement of abilities. It isn't something just mystics can do.

Even though clairvoyants do have the best possible ability, preparing, and "gift of perusing," it is surely something that can be figured out how to a degree.

Before I give you how everything people can figure out how to understand minds, it's essential to know some foundation data on mind perusing.

When you understand the science and the brain research behind psyche perusing, you will see that it is a reachable undertaking for anybody with the assurance to learn. And there are also a few deceives you can use to give the hallucination that you understand personalities.

Those stunts become considerably more helpful when you know the reality behind brain perusing.

Characteristic Mind Readers

The motivation behind why anybody can figure out how to guess thoughts is because we do it as of now.

Even though our suspicions are often off-base, it's not because the cycle of psyche perusing comes up short. We can reflect on the considerations and sentiments of people we cooperate with.

In any case, we often center our response around what we figure they will do rather than what they are revealing to us they will do. We often observe somebody's outward appearances and body language and effectively surmise that they are discouraged, debilitated, cheerful, irate, or content.

However, what happens when somebody has a decent poker face? Would we be able to at present guess thoughts without these visual signs to guide us?

Of course.

Required Skills

Truly is don't take those numerous aptitudes to understand minds. All you want is the drive to learn and the eagerness to incline toward your instinct when it mentions to you what somebody is likely reasoning or feeling right now.

You'll clearly require some training before your capacities easily fall into place for you. Be that as it might, you do not take to purchase a precious stone ball, an exceptional deck of cards, or an abnormal outfit to guess the thoughts of others.

You should have the option to free your brain from all interruptions before you endeavor to guess what someone might be thinking. For certain people, this will be the ability that sets aside the most effort to create.

Maybe you could take some yoga classes. Not exclusively will they assist you with centering your psyche and your energy. However, they will likewise give you some quality adaptability and exercise.

If you are searching for additional assets, these may help.

Tips for Beginners

If you need to figure out how to understand minds, you can follow some basic hints to kick you off. Widely acclaimed mystic Kiran Behara created these tips.

Behara's customers incorporate the absolute most extravagant and most well-known appearances in amusement and Broadway. You should begin by rehearsing these tips for your loved ones.

You should see snappy outcomes; however, it will take some time and practice to guess total outsiders' thoughts.

So here we go.

Open up Your Spirit

Notwithstanding freeing your brain from all contemplations and stresses, you should open up your energy to the people and potential outcomes around you. Try not to consider anything.

You simply need to be available at the time. Your psyche and soul should absorb the energy radiated by the people and things around you. Yoga is incredible at showing us how to do this.

However, you can learn it all alone at home in the quietness of your room.

Simply ensure people will disregard you while you start to center your musings and energy.

Seeing and Not Seeing

Free your thoughts.

Take a couple of seconds to perceive the individual sitting close to you genuinely. Make a psychological depiction of their facial structure, hair, eyes, stance, body language, and other subtleties.

However, you likewise should see everything else around that individual.

You must have a psychological segment that isolates the individual's characteristics and the other things that don't have a place with that individual. Separate the individual from the seat they are sitting in or the divider behind them. These things must be envisioned with a particular goal in mind so you can feel all the energy being created around you.

Zero in on the Person

Presently you need to restore your concentration to that individual's face. Look at them legitimately without flinching for around 15 seconds. Try not to gaze too long, or you may intrude on the energy by causing the individual to feel awkward. Following 15 seconds pass, you will need to turn away.

Make a psychological image of their face and their eyes. What does their energy feel like? Sit peacefully now as you let the considerations and sentiments of that individual fill your psyche and your spirit. You have now really begun the cycle of psyche perusing.

Start a Conversation

It is the place you will reveal the contemplations and sentiments of the individual. You can pick any topic you like for discussion. Get some information about their work or their home life. The considerations that come racing into your own brain might be the same musings crossing the other individual's thoughts. You could promptly mention to the individual what you accept they are thinking. If you have a clad memory, you can store these contemplations for later to summarize your whole impression of their considerations in these meetings.

The key is to invite any contemplations that enter your psyche now. Regardless of whether those considerations are dull and irksome, you need to give the individual a precise perusing of their contemplations. So as to do that, you should keep your brain open to each chance.

Possibly you didn't have any sign before that your brother is discouraged, and this disclosure harms you. However, your brother should realize that you're presently mindful of his battles. And now you may have the option to support him. The capacity to guess thoughts will give you a ton of intensity; however, it's a brilliant force if you use it shrewdly.

Other Tips

There is other advice you can use to increase these tips. When you increment your capacities to zero in on others' musings and sentiments, you can use more tips to give you an away from what goes on in other people's psyches.

These tips will build your odds of progress and knock the socks off of your companions, family, and outsiders you meet in the city.

Passionate Intelligence

If you realize the individual you're conversing with, you can inquire whether they feel similar feelings you're feeling. You'll show restraint toward this. Numerous people aren't truly adept at naming their feelings. They may feel furious when they're truly simply worried.

They could feel apprehensive when they're simply prepared to proceed onward to something different. If the individual you converse with concurs with the feelings, you sense, inquire whether they can sort out any reasons they may be feeling thusly.

Finally, you can start to offer recommendations on what they ought to do close to intensify or diminish these sentiments. They will be flabbergasted at your premonition and acknowledgment.

It may sound more like psychiatry than mystic brain perusing. However, it's one of the key approaches to build up your regular aptitudes.

Create Keen Listening Skills

What do all incredible communicators share practically speaking? They should be acceptable to audience members.

When somebody talks, be totally at the time with them. Try not to tune in for having the option to react. Tune in to the other individual with the goal that you can measure and understand all that they are stating. Yet, you should likewise tune in to what they're not saying too. If somebody isn't anticipating the remainder of their day, there must be a purpose behind that. Cautious listening will assist you in revealing those reasons and make them known to the individual. So as to succeed, you'll have to figure out how to listen more than you talk some of the time. Listening is the manner in which you find out about people and their feelings.

Try Not to Ignore Emotions

The explanation people need compassion today is because they decide to. Throughout each day, we are told to disregard our emotions to complete our work. Then put on a solid face for the world.

The more we overlook our emotions, the snappier they disappear. Rather than considering the new email from the chief or what you'll have for supper later, consider how you feel. As per proficient mystics, the more you can react to your own emotions, the more you will have the option to peruse and react to other people's sentiments and considerations in your life.

Guessing thoughts is something everybody can do and isn't only something for proficient mentalists and mystic peruses. You probably won't experience a lot of accomplishment from the outset, yet you can accomplish incredible advancement with training. Absolutely never utilize your new capacities to increase a bit of leeway over another person.

If you can peruse their feelings incredibly well, you may have the option to utilize that to get your direction. Utilize your capacities to help people. Brain peruses can be extraordinary companions and emotionally supportive networks for people who simply need to vent.

You have probably thought about how things would be if you could guess other people's thoughts. A few individuals utilize their instinct for this, yet if you are not all that discerning, there is just a single decision left: reckoning out how to peruse people's body language.

We get over 55% of data through nonverbal correspondence. Allan Pease, an Australian body language master, expounded on this. Emulates, motions and other body developments can expose an individual and mention to you what they truly think or feel.

Chapter 2. Myths About Body Language

We are going to deal with some commonly harbored myths about body language and bust them to paint for you the real picture.

Body Language is Mostly Communication

Imagine having to understand what your friends say by muting your ears and simply watching their body language. Of course, you will fail at it! And odds are you will hate it too! If the world were to go mute and deaf all of a sudden and the only available form of communication left was body language. The entire planet would collapse within a matter of a few hours.

You cannot rely solely on body language to understand a person's behavior. Body language is only one form of communication and not even a major one. It is assistance to words and not the main player in the game. You cannot trust body language to help you understand what a person is saying without listening to their words. However, you can get a good or bad impression of their approach. It is a combination of communication skills that allows you to make your own decision about the honesty or reliability of the person with whom you are communicating. If you do give a clear message that you are honest by keeping your shoulders straight and looking your fellow speaker in the eye, you give a better impression than those who look downward and appear not to be taking much notice of what is being said.

Liars Avoid Eye Contact

One of the oldest myths about body language is that criminals try to avoid eye contact. Imagine if our prison system was based on the mere theory that everyone who avoided eye contact was a criminal. More than half of us would be rotting behind bars if that were the case. It is a fundamental principle of criminology and body language combined that those who lie find it hard to establish eye contact. However, an entire cult of criminals is so hardened and brazen that they have understood the art of lying and have no shame from marinating in eye contact.

They could lie about what they ate in the morning and still look straight into your eyes. Not just that, some of the notorious ones could lie to the extent of misleading and manipulating you to overthink and stress yourself out. The myth that those who have done something wrong would avoid eye contact is a thing of the past.

You can tell from the eyes the level of nervousness of the person with whom you are talking. If their eyes are constantly on the move, this is a good indication that they are not relaxed.

People Who Talk Too Fast Are Liars

Again, another one of those judgmental myths. When people talk fast, it does not mean that they are telling you lies all the way. It is true that some individuals do really talk fast when they are lying—but it does not mean the same the other way around. It depends on the context. Sometimes people talk fast because they are excited about what they are chatting about. Sometimes, that is just the way that they talk.

Maybe they are in a hurry and are trying to drive an important point home. That will force them to speak at a rapid pace and try to convey a message as soon as possible. Not all people who talk too fast are liars. The other thing to bear in mind is that some people are naturally fast talkers. They may have learned that way and may not be that articulate at getting their message across. Often, I have asked people to slow down when they talk in this way, but you will always have people whose level of nervousness comes into their speech flow. It doesn't mean they are lying or trying to hide something. It does mean that they have an inbuilt nervousness about public speaking. Use another body language in conjunction with fast speech to get a more accurate picture of the person.

Crossed Arms Is A Negative Sign

Another very commonly held myth is that crossed arms signify negativity of some kind. Generally, it so happens that in a group discussion, it is considered hostile to cross your arms and not participate in the ongoing discourse. However, crossed arms could mean a lot of other things, each as possible as the next.

Those watching a theatre play and sitting in the front row usually cross their arms in order to establish a sort of barricade between the artists and themselves. In such a case, the front row people feel vulnerable being exposed to the play from such a close angle, and crossing their arms is a form of shielding themselves. If you are in a state where those you are talking to are in a similar situation, such as a lecture room, then crossed arms can simply be doing the same thing. In a situation where manual work is being done, crossed arms may just be the speaker's way of relaxing himself between jobs. However, it still shows defensiveness and a lack of openness to other opinions for a public speaker.

Smiling While Speaking Is an Indicator of Honesty

You must have seen a public speaker employing this method. They tend to smile more when they speak rather than in other situations. Smiling conveys a feeling of security and honesty. However, most of these public speakers are so seasoned that they have mastered the art of smiling to the extent where they naturally smile while addressing a crowd. It is not plastic, but it is not genuine either. The process of smiling while speaking to a crowd has become so ingrained in their system that they cannot help but sprout a smile every time they climb a podium. However, Smiling is not a sure indicator of honesty, as is evident from development-promising politicians who are all smiles right before an election starts.

You will start to identify the difference between a genuine smile and that which would be summed up as "smarm" in order to try and charm an audience into liking a speaker who is not particularly likable. Smarm is the kind of smile that is forced, and when you are talking to others, you can generally recognize one from the other.

Fumbling Is A Sign of Lying

Not necessarily! Some people fumble naturally and have been diagnosed with the medical condition of stuttering from the very beginning. If you remember well, you will recall that we talked about how a lot of factors go into deciding the correct inference about a person's body language behavior.

While we enlisted only five of them, body language myths go on running for three miles at a stretch. It is vital to comprehend that body language is not the ultimate tool for deciphering people's true intentions and emotions. Sometimes, the tool of body language fails miserably. It is not in all circumstances that you can employ body language to give you the most accurate results.

If you assume it to be the ultimate mind reading weapon for you, you are in for a great shock. As it has been mentioned before, consider all the factors possible before applying the tool of body language to decode a person's behavior.

Body language should not be read in a vacuum. There must always be context surrounding a particular body behavior. You are undertaking it all erroneous if you isolate one instance of behavior and decode it. That is a method that will lead you to definite failure. Instead of that, try to observe body language patterns in the surroundings they are created in. Before jumping to conclusions based on one instance, understand that there may be a lot of reasons a person behaves the way they behave. Often times, it is the ongoing situation that makes a person act in a certain way.

With a female, you have to take into account the mood swings the fairer sex is subjected to on account of monthly instances of losing a reasonable amount of blood (menstruation). There could be regional factors too. Most people have their moods on a roller coaster. Mood swings are as common as cupcakes, and you have to acknowledge that people are not constant. Change is the only constant. I may not be the same person today as who I was yesterday. It is, in fact, a good sign that people change for only change could lead to evolution, and without evolution, people would go stagnant, not just evolutionarily but also mentally. Therefore, while trying to decipher a person's true feelings and motives, try to take everything there is into account and then start decoding.

Perhaps the person that you are talking to is nervous in a situation where it would be normal to be nervous. In this case, body language can be forgiven because it's justified.

Any Nonverbal Sign Is A Message

It is one big myth that needs to be busted. Many people assume that any non-verbal sign is a basis of communication. In fact, they believe that 90% of people's communication will come from nonverbal signs. But this is not true. If you accept this to be correct, you might misinterpret things or over-rely on something that does not lead you anywhere. However, you have to practice your own skills of reading your own body language and the body language of people that you have known for a long time. Perhaps you haven't really paid much attention to this, but it's time that you did because it enables you to recognize body language that has a hidden message and that which does not.

Nose Touching Is Indicative of Lying

Nose touching is said to be a universal sign for lying. But this is not true! What if the person scratching the nose has an allergy or is on the verge of sneezing? Maybe the person is really not doing it on purpose. In fact, many people take offense when people touch their nose while speaking. If you think the other person is doing it on purpose, you can simply ask if they have a cold, which will alert them not to do it anymore.

Nose touching can mean various things. It is not a good thing to fix when you are talking to someone, although it is an area of the body that may be giving you problems. You would be better carrying a handkerchief and dealing with the problem, rather than trying to prevent it by touching your nose. Also, this area of the face may have dry skin around it, which may be the reason for the touching. You need to consider each individual case before you assume that someone is lying. In fact, this sign isn't really one of lying at all, and you would be better looking at eye movements and using them as your guide.

Chapter 3. Who Is a Manipulator?

Manipulative humans are the styles of folks that use intellectual and emotional abuse to 1-up you, normally to serve their dreams for energy or manipulate. Disdain the fact that it could be difficult to tell if a person is manipulative while you first meet them. There are numerous developments that manipulative human beings regularly show, which can assist tip you off early to this kind of behavior. It is crucial to appear out for manipulation in a relationship, friendship, or with a family member because you fall prey to a manipulator. It could become challenging to reduce yourself unfastened as soon as you have gotten exceptionally worried in their life. Even though manipulators are, in the end, egocentric, they use numerous schemes and methods to cowl this up. That is why it's so difficult to perceive a manipulative character earlier than it is too late. This list will give you an excellent knowledge of what to look out for in a manipulative man or woman. If you get one or further of these tendencies to your so-referred to as friends, you higher run for the hills. So, without ado, right here are ten bona fide developments of manipulative people you have to appear out for.

Manipulative Human Beings Play the Sufferer

Manipulative human beings are well-known for always playing the victim's function and making themselves out to be extra harmless than they may be. Frequently, they exaggerate or even make up non-public problems in order that others sense sorry for them and sympathize with them. In dating, this trait of a manipulative individual often comes out as dependency or co-dependency. The manipulator may also fake to be vulnerable or weak or want consistent assistance to pull the innocent victim profound into their existence. They do that to attract quality humans to them like a magnet, a good way to exploit later and use them to meet their own egocentric wishes and dreams. With the aid of playing the prey, the manipulator can are searching for out and damage the kindness, mortified conscience, or caring and fostering instinct of the goal. Have you ever had a pal or family member who continuously requested you to lend them money or requested you to buy matters for them, the complete time making you feel guilty for now not having completed so inside the first vicinity? You have probably been coping with a manipulative person. With a bit of luck, you determined your manner out of the entice without too much struggling.

Manipulative Humans Inform Distorted or Half-Truths

Another terrible persona trait that manipulative human beings have is mendacity or distorting reality, so they usually come outright. Fantastic instances of this behavior encompass excuse-making, suppression of important information, underestimations, exaggeration, or hypocrisy. Manipulative humans realize how to bend reality to their advantage. They'll often miss or cover facts to be able to divulge them as being a liar. Manipulators deal with all interactions as though they may ultimately visit trial, and everything they say can be held towards them. As a consequence, they frequently skirt from one place to another the problem or make unclear statements so that when faced, they are able to claim they "never stated that" or that it's miles "no longer precisely what they said."

Manipulative Humans are Passive-Competitive

A similarly demanding character trait of a manipulative man or woman is that they're more frequently than not passive-competitive. A manipulative man or woman might also use this type of behavior to get out of something or to get their manner. They may even do that to make you furious lacking outright deed of something offensive towards you. A family member or friend who frequently forgets something crucial you've got instructed them or overlooks to do something for you that you requested them to perform passive-competitive maybe to control you. It is able to seem innocent, but it's far, in fact, a form of anger, and it isn't healthful for their nicely-being or your sanity.

Manipulative Humans Will Strain You

Manipulative human beings, just like salespeople, will frequently position strain on any other individual in hopes of having you decide before you are truly prepared to. The manipulator believes that you will easily crack and deliver into their desires by using anxiety and managing them. Just like the one's actual-property schemes that stress you to behave fast with the promise of big profits that don't certainly exist, manipulative humans will do something to get you to buy into their sport or advantage a few types of aspect over you. So, be cautious of all and sundry who pressures you to offer a solution earlier than you are equipped, mainly if money is involved.

Manipulative Humans Will Guilt Trip You

A manipulative buddy or family member will often guilt journey you into doing something which you do not want to do, or vice versa, out of something which you do want to do. The underlying cause for this is there, in the long run, selfish personality. Guilt journeys encompass unreasonable blaming from the manipulator, together with concentrated on your soft spot and holding you responsible for their happiness, achievement, or disasters. The manipulator works to goal your vulnerabilities and emotional faintness to coerce you into doing what they want you to do. A manipulative person will frequently make a person they may be in close courting with feel guilty if that character isn't always available. They anticipate absolutely everyone else to assist them in coping with their issues but do nothing in return. Anyone who continually expects you to be the shoulder they cry on, however, who is in no way there for you while you want the same, is most likely a manipulative person.

Manipulative People Provide the Silent Remedy

Have you ever been given the silent remedy from a friend, boyfriend, lady friend, or family member? Probabilities are you had been managing a manipulative person. Manipulative people are bullies. One of the approaches they torment others is with the aid of alienation. Actions like disregarding one man or woman in a collection, now not permitting them to voice their evaluations, or leaving them out are immature strategies used by manipulative adults to claim their dominance. With the aid of showing these behaviors, the manipulative character believes they're coming off as self-confident and powerful. In reality, however, they've low vanity and are extraordinarily self-aware. The handiest way they understand a way to make themselves sense higher is with the aid of hurting others. The next time somebody gives you the silent remedy, don't feel horrific, approximately writing them off completely. It's miles a positive sign of a manipulator and has to be no longer taken lightly.

Manipulative People Do Not Do Anything to Remedy Troubles

Manipulators will, by no means, take the blame for anything. It additionally means that they may in no way make contributions to resolving a hassle in worry that one day they will be held accountable for their movements. A manipulator intends to skate through life while not having to step up and take duty for something. While confronted with something with the aid of a chum or family member, they will both flat out lie and say they by no means did something incorrectly or will make all varieties of justifications for his or her conduct that get them off the hook. You will frequently have many unsettled arguments with a dishonest man or woman, which isn't good. A key sign of this is that a manipulator will regularly quit a controversy or conversation that isn't going their way, without you even realizing it. It's far vital to recognize the way to address warfare well; however, the manipulator cannot do this because they're so centered on themselves and always being inside the proper. Any exact dating may be one in which each human surely needs to assist every other. In case you are coping with someone who can in no way paintings through trouble with you, there is a great hazard that they are now not the proper individual for you.

Manipulative People Choose to Play on Their Home Ground

As we have already set up, the character of a manipulative man or woman is very controlling. A manipulative character will generally insist on assembly or interacting with you in an area in which they feel extra powerful and in control of the situation. It could be their workplace, automobile, domestic, or any other residence where the manipulator senses awareness and ownership. The manipulator, in the long run, does this for two motives. One, they want to hold the upper hand with the aid of being in their consolation sector. And two, they want to weaken you via taking you out of yours. It ought not to be just bodily, both. A manipulator will attempt to take you from your comfort area emotionally and financially as well. Be cautious of everybody who's in no way willing to come out of their comfort zone for you or meet you midway. It's far never an amazing sign.

Manipulative People Rationalize Their Conduct

If ever approached about their manipulative phrases and deeds, a manipulator will make it appear as if it is not a great deal or will shift the responsibility onto someone else, someway making you sense horrific for them usually. However, it's miles, the manipulator who makes a big deal out of things. Until you say something to them approximately it, and then they fireplace every cannon they have got back at you to distract you from the principal subject matter at hand. Manipulators also don't have any empathy for the humans who've helped them and could even pass up to attack those humans, need to experience protecting, or want to cowl up one among their actions or deeds. The manipulative man or woman commonly knows that they have trouble but make it out to look like it's miles the world towards them, instead of the alternative way around. To the manipulative man or woman, not anything they do is ever wrong. Instead, it is always a person else's fault, and there's usually an excuse to rationalize why the manipulative individual said or did what they did.

Manipulative Human Beings Shake Your Confidence

Manipulators regularly cross overboard messing about with different people with the aid of the use of little blow jabs and abuses. Genuine friends ought to sense relaxed poking a laugh at each other harmlessly, but manipulative human beings continually take it a step too some distance. They try this, particularly in groups or social conditions, to undermine others and set up their dominance. Suppose you have a pal that continually leaves you feeling much less than brilliant approximately yourself. In that case, they will be a manipulator, and you ought to cease your friendship with them without delay.

Chapter 4. Dark Psychology and Women

Dark psychology is usually linked with the exploited behavior of people. These types of behavior are perceived very negatively. They often complete successfully for power and resources, and it usually highlights for men, but the samples of women with diversities can also not be neglected. The women's associative behavior that is very antisocial and the trade that hypnotizes and underestimates women's ability to receive and be evil is often taken in very fewer women exploit others. Yet, all of our population don't expect a woman to be threatening. They are often taken very positively, softly, and non-threatening. Even if the women harm, it is minimized, and women are very less responsible for the reactions. Also, they are very less held responsible for the actions, and because of the reason women even have done because the behavior is so unexpected.

It is the reason women think whatever they do, they can always gain sympathy in front of society, which is not necessary but somehow true.

Not everybody knows this dark psychology horror. It would benefit the women, or if they are aware of themselves' darker side, they are afraid of the headed monster. They often don't like to talk about this Complex topic where it is often said that women are the worst Enemies of other women and themselves.

It is very weird to listen to this and talk about it where it is. It is one of the highest growths in society nowadays. Women's empowerment is stronger than any other Era. People are more liberal and more vocal about women's empowerment.

They talk about it more openly. The topic of feminism is so wide and addressed and portrayed in such a beautiful way that everybody comes ahead to give their part and add; however, there is something inside every woman that reacts against their kind goes against their own will.

How it may not look wrong; however, the journey is not so easy, which is a lot of people say that it's a woman who breaks down another woman. Downgrading other Downgrading by Downgrading by life can be hard sometimes anywhere pulling Each Other back. We don't think of it often, and it is a very innocent reality that we are not aware of. It remains in their selves. Town selves' personality is negative, but it is demeaning and taken as negative because that is how we perceive. We know it is a fact that we experience space at every stage of life, but we don't discuss that. We should not discuss that women's empowerment is all about human behavior should be controlled. The women's darkest psychology should also be understood and taken in charge as it is taken in charge of the men. With men, women can also be harmful when it comes to this as compared to men.

Gossiping

There is no boundary set by dark psychology for the people. That's the same with the woman. The backbiting and the gossiping nature are the women's basic nature; it has no boundaries that are defined fun in doing so ever they don't care if anybody sentiments are being hurt.

In contrast, they are being hurt. Women tend to talk so disgustingly about other women they find entertaining; however, it is very shameful because they don't understand how much attention-seeking. It is often taken as a trait of women; however, they don't understand how attention-seeking and how embarrassing it gets, no matter if people are enjoying it, but it still looks really bad. Gossiping might look fine but can ruin another person's reputation because nobody is born a perfectionist, and nobody is born Evil. They are good on the inside; however, if a person is spreading rumors about someone, it can ruin the reputation and affect them similarly, it can of the people themselves.

It is right to be fully solved. They are being offended because if a person is gossiping, for example, if they are gossiping and confronted about their bad habit, they lose control. It does not mean that they stop doing it because it is not bound. They won't do it that openly but they would still do it is because they feel there is nothing wrong with it, and once they are pinpointed for it, they would start to pull away from people instead of abandoning this habit of themselves. They are not that trustworthy to give out secrets to them, and they can also forget someone. When women gossip, they don't know when to stop and what to say, and it can hurt someone genuinely. It gives out negative energy from them. One of the biggest things that women associated with dark psychology give out so many negative Vibes from them that are not our society is used to looking at the home. When they have them too, they always think that they would be that sweet child of people when they are not.

Bad Wording

Usually, females criticize others without giving it a thought, which doesn't take charge of everything. A woman is working to make another woman let down, and they don't feel sorry for it. Older women are bringing down the younger ones; younger ones do it to the old ones. It is an unhealthy practice overall. The funny thing is that whatever they say is so easily digestible to the people that they don't even ask them to shut up then and there. The most common practice of this is in every household between a mother in law and daughter in law relation and even the value educated people tend to do it and the thing that is the part of human nature. However, they don't understand that it can lead to something very aggressive, and still, they don't stop or refrain from doing so.

Glaring

Women are born with the most beautiful eyes, and so are men. The woman is praised for the eyes throughout their life, but it is one of the women's most typical characteristics. They glare others to their soul and give out dirty looks to everybody around them, and it is an incoming threat in general.

We often talk about bringing changes in women's empowerment forever. They can do anything that brings joy to them, and they would judge another woman by clearing at the measure; it would make them feel any better.

But they do it so the other person can feel very uncomfortable and they find betterment in doing so and they would laugh out loud, later on thinking about it. It is a very belittle characteristic of every woman; however, they don't want to help the darker side of the personality, so as a result, they don't stop doing it.

Insecure and Jealous

Women are extremely unconfident as compared to men. The same thing arises when they fear losing anyone they are attached to or something they want badly. They are very fragile, and in that situation, they suffer more emotional jealousy than any other, and it is found in any age of the women regardless of how old they are, and they can do anything to for it. They don't want to lose someone they love no matter what happens. Women react to certain situations, and insecurity and jealousy are quite common in them; however, insecurity becomes an extreme obsession if it is not taken care of.

Comparison and Competition

It sometimes happens that people are very competitive. These are the words in the personality that bring out the best outcome in people, especially women. It gets negative when they demoralize and destabilize and push Each Other down when there is a cold war among them. It just comes with a very competitive nature and then compares them with other women irrespective of any relationship and friendship. It happens quite frequently, which is why we live in a place where there is so much competition going on. Everything is going so digital the competition becomes natural; however, there are two types of competition.

There are one healthy competition and one unhealthy competition among competitions, and women are competing against Each Other. They don't look at the outcomes and what it will bring, which is why it brings out an unhealthy competition between them that brings out the worst in them. It is always necessary to hold the Horses of the hidden and powerful demons, working on the dark side. They are always competing, and they need to know that everything is temporary, and harming anybody while working to get something is not something great to do.

Belittling

The darker side of every human being gives them the feeling that they are superior to others, and they have nothing to do in their life. When that happens to them is that they start thinking that the world revolves around them. They try to belittle others because it is very easy to do so instead of showing gratitude to them, and they do anything to make others wrong. When they are criticized or shown the reality, they won't do anything to make it better. Instead, they always put other people down and want to preserve their superiority over others. They always want to have a high status in front of everybody, so what they think is necessary to do so to look better and everybody, whereas they are just making a fool of themselves, which is quite toxic.

Women cannot usually understand this behavior. People must admit and examine themselves, which is the above dark psychology because it can disturb women's life and people around them because not every woman is like this.

But there are certainly some women whose darker side is more powerful than the other side of their life. Every human being has a dark and light inside. It happens women's approach is how they see different things. Similarly, when feminism has become the town's talk, women should understand that there is a light side of feminism and a dark side of feminism. There is so much more related to the community, especially when their traditional ideas on the concept of femininity. It targets women in a particular way of living in a particular way of acting; however, some women do not agree with the feminism idea and its criteria. They never oppose their beliefs, which are that living like a nice girl is not enough. It may be a pleasant experience to see what it takes to take the whole of the darker side. Still, they need to understand that feminine energy is such a beautiful gift for women to experience by the substrates woman to be only the underside of themselves. They are unaware of how the direct energy works, but they keep falling into a pit hole.

Chapter 5. Techniques of Dark Psychology

Reverse Psychology

A first tactic that a dark persuader can use is reverse psychology. This technique consists of assuming a behavior opposite to the desired one. It is with the expectation that this "prohibition" will arouse curiosity and induce the person to do what is desired.

Some people are known to be like boomerangs. They refuse to go in the direction they are sent to but take the opposite route. It works better when someone else is educated and chooses instinctively rather than thinking about things. They can introduce the intention to do X thing when they suggest the 'do not do X.' When you claim that you will do it, you may wonder whether you will do so.

A dark persuader can use this type of behavior because it is a weakness that the victim has. Take an example of a friend who loves to eat junk food at any opportunity he gets. The dark persuader knows this and will suggest that they eat because it will be good for him, knowing that the friend will choose fast food, anyway.

Reverse Psychology can be used in sales techniques when dealing with a difficult customer.

In this case, the seller can say: "this is a product for rich people. I don't know if it can work for you because it costs a lot of money".

So, the seller is like saying: "I don't want to sell it to you. It's not the right product for you since you can't afford it," just because reverse psychology leads the person to want the product even more.

Masking True Intentions (Door in the Face)

Masking true intentions is another tactic a dark persuader will use to get what they want. A dark persuader will disguise their true intentions from their victims and can use different approaches depending on their victims and the surrounding circumstance. One approach a dark persuader can use is using two requests consecutively because people find it hard to refuse two requests in a row. Take this example; a manipulator wants $500 from their victim. The dark persuader will begin by explaining why they need $1000 while stating what will happen if they cannot come up with that amount. The victim may feel guilt or compassion but will kindly explain to the manipulator that they cannot lend the amount because, quite frankly, it's more than they can manage to give when the persuader lessens the amount to $500, which was what they wanted from the beginning. They will attach the amount with some emotional reason where the victim will be unable to refuse the second request. The dark persuader walks away with the original sum, and the victim is left confused about what took place.

The Blame Game

If the manipulator wants to make you do something against your will, he will have a better chance of getting that behavior by making you feel guilty. Blame is one of the most powerful manipulation techniques known to humankind. Guilt can be used to manipulate people by making them feel inferior to the help and support they have received, or it can also be used to make others feel inadequate for a "condition" they have. Think about all those times you hear people say, "things would be different if I weren't sick." It is one of the most rudimentary ways to make someone feel guilty, but it is very powerful. Besides, you might hear others say things like, "remember when you need my help? Now I need your help." It is a clear attempt to convince someone to follow the manipulator's intentions.

Putting the Other Person Down

Through this technique, we try to make the other person feel less capable than he is. For example, you find every pretext to point out to the victim when makes a mistake, and you do it repeatedly to throw off his self-esteem. A person with low self-esteem is manageable and controllable, therefore manipulable. This way, the manipulator will feel in control of the situation.

When a person tries to manipulate you with this technique, remember that they will attack your identity, telling you phrases like "you are incapable" instead. They will never tell you, "you are behaving like an incapable person." To react to this technique, you have to detach yourself from this psycho-trap. Instead, you need to think that the person is judging your behavior at that moment and not your identity.

Leading Questions

It involves the dark persuader questions that trigger some response from the victim. A persuader may ask a question like, "do you think that this person could be so mean?" This question implies that the person will be bad in one way or another. An example of a non-leading question is, "What do you think about that person?" When we use leading questions, dark persuaders ensure that they use it carefully. Dark persuaders know that when the victim feels like they are being led to trigger a certain response, they will become more resistant to being persuaded.

When the dark persuader feels that the victim has to be aware that he or she is being led, they will immediately change tactics and return to asking the leading questions only when the victim has come down.

Fatigue Inducement

The impact of mental fatigue on perceptual, emotional, and motivational factors are complex. In exhaustion, special effects can be assumed to rely on the operation's essence that causes fatigue. This study investigated the impact of exhaustion on different activities based on working memory demands on brain function and efficiency. The results showed that driving quality was not impaired by exhaustion. The effects of fatigue on novelty therapy depended on the mental requirements for the task that caused fatigue.

Creating an Illusion

Create exaggeratedly high or unrealizable expectations. But presenting and selling them in such a powerful, persuasive, and tempting way for you that you'll end up believing it.

With this technique, it is likely to make the victim see the most beautiful future so that she will be willing to do anything to make it happen, even spend a lot of money. The goal is to make people "daydream" to give them the hope of living their lives to the full.

Commitment and Congruity

Highly skilled and sophisticated manipulators know that building trust capital is essential, especially when building a long-term approach. Think about the most sophisticated conmen you can imagine. These are individuals who take time, often years, building up trust around them through congruent behavior so that others can tumble into their trap.

At first, no one suspects the least bit in this individual as they have earned everyone's trust. As they gain more and more trust, they can use that trust capital to deceive others. It gives them some leeway in case they slip up. Given their track record, they will always have the benefit of the doubt.

This tactic is not common in less-sophisticated manipulators as it requires a great deal of dedication. Impulsive individuals will never be able to pull this off as they focus more on short-term rather than long-term gain. Through this type of tactic, many manipulators can build a name for themselves in their chosen domain. However, they are often exposed. When this occurs, the world is shocked to learn that who they thought was a pillar of their community was actually a manipulator.

One good example of this is a cheating spouse. An individual may cheat on their spouse for years without them noticing what's going on. Then, one day, the manipulator makes a mistake, whatever it is, and they are exposed. The shock that comes to the victim is overwhelming.

The reason why this tactic always backfires is due to the fact that the manipulator doesn't know when to stop. The longer they go without getting caught, the more they think the con will last forever. History has taught us that everyone gets caught eventually.

Reciprocity

It is the classic "quid pro quo," in other words; you scratch my back, I'll scratch yours. However, the victim doesn't know the extent to which they are being manipulated.

A great example of this can be found with informants.

When a manipulator wishes to extract information from someone, they may offer tidbits of information of their own in the hopes of motivating the victim to furnish the information the manipulator is looking for. However, the key to making this tactic work is that the manipulator must give information of little or no value while extracting information that may be profitable.

Manipulators also use this tactic when doing favors. They build up capital and then "call-in" favors. While this may seem like it's perfectly reasonable, it is a manipulation tactic as the manipulator doesn't do favors out of the goodness of their heart. They do it so that they can have people they can rely on in times of need. Alternatively, they can resort to guilt or even blackmail if the other party refuses to cooperate.

Scarcity and Demand

Often, manipulators realize that they have something, or at least have access to something, that people really want. When this occurs, they can manipulate those around them by creating a false illusion of scarcity.

Earlier, we talked about how advertisers generally use phrases such as "limited quantities available" or "while supplies last." These phrases have become so cliché that no one really buys into them anymore.

Yet, manipulators can make this work by creating a sense that there really is a scarcity of a product or service. Some of the more outright, devious ways of pulling this off are by planting fake informants who spread lies. When these lies spread, people may begin to panic and flock to get the products and services in question.

Another way of pulling this off is by spreading rumors on social media. Some people fall for it, and some don't. In the end, the goal is to create enough confusion so that no one is able to tell the difference.

Lastly, manufacturers may go as far as hoarding supplies in order to create an artificial scarcity. It has worked well throughout history. In fact, it's worked so well that it is illegal in most countries. Still, manufacturers can pull this off by controlling the entire supply chain of their products. So, any disruption along that line will cause scarcity, thereby creating panic in people. The manufacturers themselves are not responsible for the scarcity as they are not the ones who technically caused the issue.

Consensus

This tactic consists of setting situations in such a manner that people will agree to them regardless of what it is. Governments do this all the time. For instance, they know that no one will ever agree to a tax hike. Yet, they frame the situation in such a manner that if people wish to continue receiving government benefits, they need to accept the tax hike as there is no other way to fund it. So, people reluctantly accept the tax hike out of fear of losing their benefits.

Chapter 6. Practical Exercises For Mind Control Prevention

The real question here is why, in the first place, would anyone want to control your mind? Some people may not want to check out some of these exercises because they feel like there would be no reason for a person to try to control their minds in the first place, but you must know that there are many reasons people may want to control your mind. Some of the reasons why people would want to control your mind include:

- They want you to get something for them: It may be money, documents, or any other thing. They have chosen you because they know you are the only one that can get it for them. As such, you become their mind control project. There are even stories of people that say that they were robbed one way or the other, but when they checked the security tapes, the people who called the police were the robbers. Sounds strange, right? A professional can get you to rob your own house and plant a bomb in there by yourself, even if you have no bomb training.

- They may want information: This is another reason why someone would want to hypnotize you. You do not necessarily need to have money for someone to need something from you. They may need access codes or maybe the names of people in a place. What they want to do with the information is a total mystery, but the thing is that you might have succeeded in telling them things that you would not normally tell them if you were not hypnotized in the first place.

Exercise 1: Do Not Keep Your Eyes in One Position

People who tend to control the minds of others can be very skilled at times. Some of them would want to use everything they can to get your attention to persuade you and control your mind at all times. When you notice that you are in the presence of someone that wants to control your mind, try as much as possible to keep your eyes in random motion. Do not let your eyes focus on one thing simultaneously, especially if that thing is something they are holding.

There are various ways a person can control your mind, and your eyes are a good gateway for that to happen. You do not want your gateway to be wide open and for you to be defenseless when someone is trying to get into your mind. When someone is trying to control your mind, and you notice, all you have to do is avoid any kind of eye contact with them.

Do not let them think that they can get to you with your eyes because when they do, they will use that technique against you almost every single time. When people like that find your weak point, they tend to exploit it no matter how many times you try to hide it. It is why you mustn't let them know what that is in the first place.

You should not do certain things when trying to avoid eye contact with the person trying to control your mind. These things are said to be very important and should not be taken for granted. Some of these things include:

- Don't let them know: You should never let the person that is trying to control your mind know that you know what he or she is doing and, most importantly. Do not let them know that you are aware of their technique because when they know that you are aware of their technique, they will tend to change it immediately, and they might still be able to get you one way or the other. If you want to be able to get out of that problem, all you have to do is act oblivious.

- Don't get distracted: Getting distracted around a person who is trying to control your mind is the last thing you want to do when it comes to avoiding them. When you want to avoid something like mind control, you need to make sure that you are alert at all times. When you are avoiding the eyes of the people who are trying to control you, you mustn't forget and mistakenly gaze at them again because that might be your downfall. Keep your mind and body alert at all times because the moment you let your guard down, they would not hesitate to take advantage of you.

If you can keep your eyes in constant random motion and at the same time avoid all these pointers, there is a good chance that no one would be able to get into your mind no matter how many times they try. You should know that some professionals would go out of their way to get to you, but if you stick to all that you need to do, you would be one of their biggest challenges. If you play your cards right, you may be able to confuse them to the point that they would have to leave you alone and go for much easier targets. How do you confuse them? When they try to get to you with your eyes, let them get to the point that they think they have almost gotten you and make them know that they are still a long way from penetrating your mind. Once they notice that the closer they are to getting to your mind, the harder it gets; they would get confused because you would become a harder nut to crack.

Exercise 2: Don't Let People Copy Your Body Language

It is probably something that you thought was far from important, but it is. If you are in the presence of a person trying to control your mind and find out the person is sitting in the way you are seated. Even the person is mirroring your movements in any way, keep it in mind that the person is somehow trying to get inside your mind. It is why it is important to mind your surroundings at all times because they could get to you just by mirroring your hand gestures.

You may not notice them doing this because they can be subtle as they possibly can. If you even come in contact with the professionals, there is a huge chance that you will not be able to find out what they are up to until it is too late to go back. It is important to know that you may figure the person out if they are new in the game.

The thing is that professionals are very clean in their game, so clean that you may not know what they are doing until they are done. Still, when it comes to a rookie, you can be able to spot what he or she is doing almost immediately because they are not as clean as the professionals. A professional would mirror your movements and gestures very quietly, meaning that you would never catch them doing it. Still, a rookie, on the other hand, may tend to change his or her gestures immediately. You change yours. That's right; there is a huge giveaway. When you notice something like that happening around you, know that the person you are dealing with is a big-time rookie, and all you have to do is to mess with them and have fun with it. You can change your gestures and movements as often as possible and watch them get confused and break down.

There are certain things that you do not want to be doing. Especially when a person is trying to mirror your movements in any way at all, these things include:

- Never sit in one place: This is probably the last thing you want to do, especially if the person trying to mirror you is right in front of you. When you are in the presence of someone like that, all you have to do is keep moving around. You do not need to move around like a mad person. If not, they would know that you have made them.

Just move around casually like you have no idea what is going on around you, and if you can be in as many places as possible and still make as many gestures as possible, there is a good chance that they are not going to be able to see where you are going. Some of them may get so frustrated. Even decide to get your attention by subtly standing in front of you. It is so that you forget what exactly you are doing. But when they do, you can always change your gestures over and over again. It is to mess with their heads.

- Mind your surroundings: This may be hard for some people because many people find it hard to mind their surroundings, no matter how long you try to teach them. They are more focused on the things happening right in front of them and fail to see the things happening around them.

If you are that kind of person, getting into your mind would be a piece of cake because if you want to notice someone trying to get you, you have to be aware of your surroundings with every chance you get. Do not see something strange on the road or in your house and just let it go like that. Try as much as possible to investigate even if you do not get there by yourself.

- The bottom line to all of this is that if you know what is going on around you, you would be able to tackle and address it before it becomes too late, and when you address it early enough, there is absolutely no way that a person can easily control your mind.

It is imperative to know that these tips would not work for everyone, and you must also know that you would not be able to get the best results out of this if you practice it repeatedly. You need to practice in this context because there are many skilled mind control specialists out there, and you need to be on your game at all times. You do not need to sit down thinking that no one can get into your mind just because you have succeeded in successfully spotting one or two of them coming your way. There is a good chance that you will meet a person that is more than a professional. These mind control specialists do not need to get close to you to know what you are doing and control your mind.

Some of these kinds of people can come to you, and the only thing they have to do is to say a word to you, and that word may be able to trigger some series of events, and before you know it, you are under the control of someone you just met.

Chapter 7. Touch As a Form of Body Language

We engage in touching routinely. We commonly shake hands as greetings or assign to signal shared understanding. Touch, as a form of communication, is called haptics. For children, touch is a crucial aspect of their development. Children that do not get adequate touch have developmental issues. Touch helps babies cope with stress. At infancy, touch is the first sense that an infant responds to.

Functional Touch

At the workplace, touch is among effective means of communication, but it is necessary to keep it professional or casual. For instance, handshakes are often exchanged within a professional environment and can convey a trusting relationship between two people. Pay attention to the nonverbal cues that you are sending next time you shake someone's hand. Overall, one should always convey confidence when shaking another person's hand, but you should avoid being overly-confident. A firm pat on the back communicates praise and encouragement. Remember, people have varied reactions to touch as nonverbal communication. For instance, an innocent touch can make another person feel uncomfortable or frightened.

Touch can become particularly complicated when touch is between a boss and a subordinate. Generally, those in power will utilize touch with subordinates to reinforce the hierarchy of the workplace. It is usually not acceptable for it to occur the other way around. For this reason, you should make sure to be careful even in the instance of using the most trivial of touches and resolve to enhance your communication techniques with your juniors. A standard measure is that it is better to fail but remain on the side of caution. Functional touch includes being physically examined by a doctor and being touch as a form of professional massage.

Social Touch

In the United States, a handshake is the most common way one engages in social touching. Handshakes vary from culture to culture, though. In some countries, kissing one or both cheeks are more common than a handshake. In the same interactions, men will allow a male stranger to touch them on their shoulders and arms, whereas women feel comfortable being touched by a female stranger only on the arms. Men are likely to enjoy a female stranger's touch while women tend to feel uncomfortable with any touch by a male stranger. Equally important, men and women process touch differently, which can create confusing and awkward situations. One should be respectful and cautious. For instance, while you stand close to a stranger on an elevator, it is not acceptable to stand so close to them that you contact him or her.

Friendship Touch

The types of touches allowed between friends vary depending on the context. For instance, women are more receptive to touching female friends compared to their male counterparts. Touch is different depending on the closeness of the family and the sex of the family member. Displays of affection between friends are almost always appreciated and necessary, even if you are not a touchy person. One should be willing to get out of their comfort zone and offer their friend a hug when struggling. Helping others enliven their moods is likely to uplift your moods as well.

Intimacy Touch

In romantic relationships, touches that communicate love play a critical role. For instance, the simplest of touches can convey a critical meaning, such as holding hands or placing your arm around your partner, which communicates that you are together. According to recent communication studies, adults place more emphasis on nonverbal cues than verbal cues when communicating. In the earlier stages of dating, men tend to initiate physical contact in line with societal norms, but in later stages, women initiate contact. Women place more premiums on touch compared to men, and even the smallest of gestures can help calm women. They were upset.

Arousal Touch

Arousing touches are elicited by intense feelings and are only acceptable when mutually agreed upon. Arousal touches are meant to evoke pleasure and involve kissing, hugging, flirtatious touching, and are often intended to suggest sex. One should be careful about their partner's needs. One can greatly improve their communication skills and relationships by considering the nonverbal messages you send via touching behavior.

Additionally, our sense of touch is intended to communicate clearly and quickly. Touch can elicit subconscious communication. For instance, you instantly pull away from your hand when touching something hot even before you consciously process. In this manner, touch constitutes one of the quickest ways to communicate. Touch, as a form of nonverbal communication, is an instinctive form of communication. In detail, touch conveys information instantly and causes a guttural reaction. Completely withholding touch will communicate the wrong messages without your realization.

Ways of Improving Touch in Appropriate Contexts

Pat Someone on the Back When You Grant Them Praise

If your colleague or friend has graduated, earned a promotion, or married, then pat them on the back. Giving a pat suggests that you are happy with the person and are encouraging them. Touch has a therapeutic value that relaxes the mind and the body and helps an individual feel secure and appreciated. At school, you must have felt valued and loved if you were patted on the back.

Initiate Discussions with a Touch to Create Cooperative Relationships

Studies have established that touching a person increases their willingness to cooperate and work with others. They were establishing physical contact with an individual that you wish to initiate a conversation with can help. Sometimes the target person may not realize that you touched them but will register subconsciously and establish a bond.

Extend the Handshakes

Shaking hands shows confidence and simplicity in interacting with others. Touch helps build trust between two people. Make your handshakes firm when shaking hands with people. It is also necessary to remember that some health conditions may make one shy away from shaking hands, and this includes hyperhidrosis, which makes the palms of the person sweat. With sweaty hands, the individual is likely to shun handshakes, and this has little to do with the context of the conversation.

Adjust the Touch-Type Concerning Context

As indicated, touch is highly contextual. For instance, the Japanese do not favor shaking hands, and a person in this environment will avoid shaking hands at all costs. In the American context, shaking hands is encouraged. For this reason, one should adjust their touch-type depending on the contexts. It might be welcome to continuously hold your partner's hands while the same is creepy when talking to a stranger or to a colleague at the workplace.

Another form of touch is tickling, mostly reserved for lovers, parents versus children, and peers. For instance, a mother may tickle her baby, which is a therapeutic touch and is permissible. On the other hand, children of the same age set may tickle each other, which is permissible. However, it is inappropriate to tickle an adult when you are not lovers, or the relationship between you and them is formal.

Touch as a Form of Abuse

Expectedly, there is a thin line between permissible touch and physical abuse. If not, certain one should avoid initiating touch unless fully certain its meaning to the target person. Pushing someone or pinching someone is considered a form of physical abuse. Kicking or striking someone as well as strangling, are forms of physical abuse.

- Touch as a game

In some contexts, a touch is a form of the game, especially teasing. Touch as a form of the game should only happen where the participants are peers and are receptive to it. For instance, your friend or classmate may blindfold your eyes with the palms of their hands from behind. The participants in this tease may touch each other. For instance, the blinded person may try to feel your arms or head to guess the person's identity. In this form of touch, the scope of teaching allowed is large and may be equivalent to that of lovers.

Chapter 8. Facial Expression As a Form of Body

Facial Expressions and Physiognomy

We want to understand by facial expressions all phenomena that we can observe in the face of a human being. By this, we mean both facial features, eye contact, and viewing direction, as well as psychosomatic processes, such as pale. Finally, we also include entire head movements with such. As a nodding, oblique (the latter, depending on the context, of course, the attitude can be assigned).

In general, we are concerned with the evaluation of congruence signals. As long as the facial expressions match the verbal utterances, we usually do not take them very well. When the incongruity is strong, it attracts even the most inexperienced. But the experienced can take note of a variety of facial expressions to perceive even slight disturbances or incipient incongruence (or, of course, first signs of relief, approval, etc.). Often only a barely perceptible grin indicates that someone is making a joke. Or it may be that a (questioning) raised eyebrow is the only indication of contradiction when the other one says, "Yes, I understand what you mean."

At this point in the seminar, the question often arises of how far one can manipulate his non-linguistic signals to what extent z.

For example, it would be possible not to let it be noted whether one grasps or approves of something?

Answer: Of course, anyone can learn to influence his body language to a degree.

However, it is particularly difficult to get the facial muscles under control. So, you can often observe that someone looks outwardly calm because he has learned to control his hands (for example, by intertwining his fingers to prevent him from playing around nervously). Nevertheless, an inner restlessness (if any) will express itself, and most likely, in the face. Why is the manipulation of our facial muscles so difficult? The word "manipulate" includes the word manus (lat., The hand). However, to be able to handle something skillfully, you have to know it well. We do not know enough about our facial muscles to get a grip on them. In general, we do not know how we look or how we affect others. Try it (right now) yourself! Check your facial expression.

A real experiment on this would look like this: You get a small pocket mirror, which you always have at hand shortly. Now and then, you will try first to feel your expression and then immediately see it in the mirror. Ask yourself before and while you look in each case: "How do I look now? How do I now seem to others?" (Or how would I act on others now?)

You will experience very exciting surprises, although they are not positively fascinating for everyone. Some people are horrified when they realize how often they have a discontented, disgruntled look around their mouths and eyes that they did not even realize! However, the less you know about his facial expression, the less you really know him, the less you can, of course, also manipulate him. That is, you have it.

A second mini-experiment that you can do immediately confirms this. After reading the instruction, close your eyes briefly and try to relax your face, especially the lips and chin, as much as possible. Observe and feel consciously what it feels like.

Stop.

Now three questions:

- Have you achieved relaxation?

- Have you got a feel for feeling your facial muscles?

- Were your lips laid together loosely?

If you answered yes to the last question, then you have confirmed what FELDENKRAIS (29) means when he says:

"How is it that such an important part of the body as the lower jaw is constantly held up? Muscles that work while we are awake, without even the slightest sensation that we are doing something to hold the jaw up?

To drop it, you even have to learn how to apply the muscle inhibitor. Suppose one tries to relax his lower jaw so much that he falls through his own weight and opens his mouth completely, so you will wonder how difficult that is. If it finally succeeds, one will notice changes in the facial expression and in the eyes. It will probably also be noticed later that one usually presses his lower jaw upwards or keeps his mouth firmly closed. "

Did the little experiments teach you a little about how little you normally know about your facial muscles? Every actor who deals (or mainly) with pantomime knows the difficulties associated with the conscious creation of a desired facial expression.

Knowing the difficulties of manipulating one's facial expressions is essential if we want to control our facial expressions. With too much control, if they succeed, resulting in a robotic, non-living expression! But Information is also essential if we want to interpret the signals of others. Since the other person is just as unaware of his facial expressions, one can rely on the facial expressions in general quite well.

By the way, the study of the facial expression is divided into two areas, the facial expression itself and the physiognomy. Under the latter, one understands not the momentary, ever-changing expression but the facial features that a person has in general. I call that the "facial expression." If a person often expresses displeasure by squeezing his lips and lowering his mouth's corners, it does not surprise him if he has so-called mis-wrinkles after years. These are deeply scored "lines" that run down from the corners of the mouth. Anyone who looks at the young SCHOPENHAUER's face and then compares it with the old image can clearly see this (see also: "the compressed mouth").

The physiognomy also includes an interpretation of the facial or nasal form. Although the separation from the phrenology, which GALL (94) founded, is not clear. We will not practice physiognomy or phrenology.

Nevertheless, we cannot help but, for example, to register deep scored wrinkles when we consciously perceive. But even such a signal alone has no significance. To be sure, the wrinkling itself is unmistakable, so that we know that this man must often have his lips pinched and the corners of his mouth lowered, but we do not know why this happened. Of course, it may be that this human being is a "Griesgram" who does not like anything. But it may just as well be that this person has suffered a serious illness or a hard fate. Think of persons who have lost a loved one, to people who have spent years in concentration camps or to those who have been tortured (as is commonplace in certain parts of the world today), etc.

It has become customary to assume the following subdivision:

- Forehead area (including the eyebrows)
- Midface, i.e., eye, nose, and cheek area (for most authors, including the upper lip)
- Mouth (or lower lip) and chin area

The Forehead Area

It is believed that the forehead, with its wrinkles and eyebrows, provides information about processes of thinking and analyzing. Although this opinion seems to be a remnant of GALL's phrenology (94), I still hold the forehead's statements applicable. Nevertheless, of course, there is the demand for caution on the part of "scientificity" of such interpretations.

The Midface

The eye, nose, and cheek area are also referred to as the sense of sight. Most authors include the upper lip because they make more nuanced detail statements than we do. We usually only speak of the Lips or from the mouth, so that it is not so important in our frame, where you want to draw the border exactly.

The sense of sight is said to give us clues about taking on the outside world. It is because the eyes are the "window to the world." But they are rightly called the "window to the soul." So that we see that information from the inner life can also be seen in this area. It should also be borne in mind that the mouth also plays a key role in environmental uptake processes.

The Mouth and Chin Area

The mouth has developed from the Ur-Maw, which already has a very simple organism. It represents the relationship to the environment, in that the organism absorbs as well as eliminates it. It is easy for small children to see that they put everything in their mouths to grasp it. Therefore, it is not surprising that the mouth plays an essential role, both when it comes to not "let in" information from the environment and when one does not want to or is not allowed to express.

Next, assign the chin part (including the lower lip) the emotional and intuitive life, and, especially the chin, the assertiveness. A person who is about to assert himself vigorously will push his chin as a mimic signal. (While the assessment of the chin shape regarding the character traits of assertiveness belongs to the field of phrenology.)

And now, let's look at the interpretations of the three facial area turns.

Since we do not want to analyze the forehead's shape, we are concerned with the mimic expressions of forehead wrinkles, horizontal and vertical. Usually, horizontal wrinkles are accompanied by a lifting of the eyebrows. But there is also a barely noticeable lifting of one or both brows, which does not wrinkle.

Horizontal Forehead Wrinkles

As a rule of thumb, we can say that the horizontal forehead wrinkles indicate that the attention has been drawn heavily. However, this strong attention can have very different occasions. For example, Zeddies (94) calls the following:

- Fright.

- Anxiety.
- Obtuseness.
- Astonish.
- Amazement.
- Confusion.
- Surprise.

Again, it becomes clear that individual signals (usually) must be seen in association with others. It also applies within a category, such as facial expressions. For the forehead, wrinkles are automatically associated with the face's other muscle movements, which open eyes (or an open mouth) can lead to. Such a combination provides, for example, the following:

Horizontal wrinkles and open eyes. According to ZEDDIES (94), the two mean signals interpreted together: "The mental attitude lies in a waiting, attentive attitude to any circumstances that offer themselves to the consciousness."

Another possible combination of two mimic signals would be horizontal forehead wrinkles forming in conjunction with half-closed (= easy squinted) eyes. This combination can be observed if someone goes to great lengths to listen; in the case of the hard of hearing, for example, or in situations in which the volume of the transmitter (including technical sound sources such as a radio) is not sufficient. The vernacular describes this with the expression "the ears are pointed." However, this formulation not only describes "in a figurative sense" but also indicates physiological processes. In fact, when we tip our ears, we actually move our severely stunted ear muscles in a reflex that is pronounced in dogs, cats, and rabbits. An additional gesture and attitude change will often accompany the effort to "play" our "spoons."

Conclusion

The culture romanticizes deceptive relations so much when talking about the love that it can be hard to recognize them for what they are. We have lots of literature suggesting that genuine relationships are about fixation, that pure love is all-out, and that infatuated people have no boundaries or separate lives.

While many people romanticize the concept of a deceptive relationship, we have to realize that it is not real love. Sometimes it may trigger a dramatic storyline and tension that keeps the reader engaged, but there is no fun living through a deceptive relationship that is romantic.

You may have been warned of manipulating people and the fact that coercion and mistreatment are worrying; the facts are that being in a relationship of control and manipulation that never develops into ill-treatment can also be terrifying and dangerous. Just because somebody does not harm you physically does not mean you cannot feel pain from their actions yet.

Being dominated or put down by a partner can damage our faith, make us feel fearful of relationships in the future, and leave us feeling lost rather than comforted, with various mental and emotional injuries with which we should not be burdened.

You may be familiar with the symptoms of a negative relationship. You might have met a partner, for instance, who required you to wear only certain clothing items or did not want you to visit your friends and family.

This person might want to know where you are going, what you are doing, and why you are just a couple of minutes late. Manipulators are frequently very anxious people, allowing nervous thoughts to pass through their brains and control their actions. We channel their intense fear and anxiety into hallucinations about what you might do if you are not around them. They will think about their worst fears and what you can do to damage them, so they will assume you are doing these things when you are not around.

Such things may spur them to hate you if you are not around. Sometimes it may seem flattering to have someone so concerned about you. You might think, "It is so sweet that they always want to know where I am, and I am safe," but it is not their intention when someone is going to take great steps to control you.

Unfortunately, they are not concerned about your well-being. Therefore, the manipulators are thinking, "I need to make sure I know where this person is at all times, so they do not do something that I do not approve of." Your presence is their assurance that you are not meeting their worst fears about the bad things that you are doing to them when you are not both of you together. In this case, they will not be addressing your needs. The manipulator behaves only to serve the interests of his own.

A manipulator will never tell you that but will only be worried about improving the way they look to you. They are always going to use this technique to make sure you feel guilty. They will make you feel guilty if you do not respond for 20 minutes, instead of admitting that it is acceptable for a person not always to write back immediately. They would view you as if you did something wrong or disrespectful to them because, at the time, you were not around your phone or too busy to answer first.

Marriage should feel better, not confining, scary, or distressing, and having an accomplice will make you happier, not more sorrowful. There will be hard times in life. Your mate may not be understood, and they may not understand you. On the way to making you stronger, these challenges should be pure obstacles. There shouldn't be a healthy relationship that continuously drains you and tears you down, making you feel constantly exhausted.

Signs of a Manipulative Relationship

Most of us have had terrible things happening in our lives—enough terrible things that the prospect of a hero sweeping us off our feet and protecting us from any problems for whatever remains of our lives can sound extremely tempting. For this reason, we are sometimes looking in the wrong places for security, empathy, and care.

Reconsider whether your partner's support thoughts include stopping you from making your own decisions and living your own life. This partner secures you by assuming responsibility for your maxed-out accounts. Or perhaps speaking to a partner you have been struggling with does not pay special attention to you; they are trying to make you have no choice but to put all your faith in them and no one else.

A true partner knows they cannot protect you and what it holds from everyday life—they can just support when you need them. If you run into a money-related issue at some point, a trusted partner can help you pray an overabundance of unopened bills—give help, but do not take control of the situation. They will not take your passwords or insist that only a small amount of money per month be allowed until you have paid off all of your current debt. A right partner is going to offer help yet realize you need to manage your problems.

One typical manipulative relationship is making us feel guilty when we see friends and family members. Suppose we imagine someone trying to cut off their partner from their emotionally supportive network. In that case, we envision something similar to the contemptible husband in a movie made for TV that threatens his better half that she will never talk to her closest friend again. Nevertheless, deceptive spouses can also inconspicuously isolate you from your support network.

A shrewdly manipulative person will not outwardly discourage you from seeing your family because it can be an obvious sign that you should be running in the opposite direction. We will make the coercion more subtle, rather than slowly dragging you out of your life, rather than an outright ban. If your partner can convince you to apologize for an action that you know you have not done wrongly and that you are doing, your manipulative partner will realize that he or she can force you to do whatever they want you to do.

Each time you go out with your buddies, your partner can sulk until you blow off other friends just to save the tension. Perhaps your partner will make negative remarks about your loved ones until you begin to believe that the thoughts they have about these people are valid.

You may even have a hobby or an event you enjoy trying to get your manipulator to stop doing it. They will ensure that you know that your interest is idiotic and will ridicule you until you give it up.

The scrutiny of a controlling partner may not always appear as such. It can be framed reasonably and rationally, implying that your partner is just trying to help you. They might even tell you they are trying to help you.

At school, they will research your decisions. Some of their sentences may include: "Why do you choose to use it for your presentation? You are not thinking about what the boss will think? They are going to question your spending habits and how you are going to buy things with questions like, "Did you have to buy another shirt?" Manipulators are going to spin their words, so it is not clear that the choices you make are wrong, but a seed of doubt and insecurity is being planted.

All partners, however, examine each other periodically. Our loved ones are still supposed to look for us, and sometimes we need others to help us make choices or point out bad habits. Remember, always test this person's true purpose and determine why they had wanted you to change your actions.

Sometimes a manipulator may ask for access to your personal belongings in a relationship, but they will not grant you the same rights. We may know all your secrets, but we rarely trust you.

They are not just less likely to share, and they are not helping you.

This type of behavior demonstrates that the other person dominates. Your partner does not reserve the right to search your emails or texts or asking for your passwords because they say they are concerned that you may be cheating. There is a distinction between having insider facts and having healthy independence from your partner, and when you are in a relationship with someone, you do not have to surrender that.

Every so often, sincere couples healing from a disaster would require the weakened spouse to view each other's messages as a form of transparency. If this is not an agreement you have worked out directly with your partner, it is incorrect.

By emotional influence, coercion is all about influencing the way someone else thinks and acts. Coercion is veiled with emotion, or at least what appears to be a sort of empathy. Most of the time, this is a calculated attempt by the manipulator concerned to relate to the victim.

We must recognize the impact it has had on us to overcome this manipulation completely. If you want a healthy relationship with someone, we must look at all the ways we have been affected by their relationship. It may be the first sign that there is a manipulative relationship if that impact is negative.

Most manipulative people have four standard attributes: they know the weaknesses.

- They use your vulnerabilities against you.

- They persuade you to surrender something of yourself to serve them through their quick plots.

- If a controller triumphs in manipulating you, he will likely repeat the crime until the mistreatment is stopped.

- They are going to have a lot of different reasons for keeping you around and controlling you.

One might just be because a past relationship damages them. We may have confidence issues that have made it difficult for them to be transparent and consider other partners. This situation can make them feel like they need to manipulate you to keep you loyal to them.

Understand Your Rights in a Relationship

It can be difficult to understand how to get out when someone is in the midst of an abusive relationship.

Manipulators are good at creating uncertainty, so they can also avoid blame for trying to control others instantly. Recalling your rights is the way to ensure that you are safe.

These are the things you completely have the right to take away and should never allow another person to take away. If you can remember these consistently, manipulation will be easier to confront as it happens, and it will be easier to recognize when a conversation may be toxic.

Then again, you may give up these rights if you convey vulnerability to other people. Our common, main human rights are the following: you deserve respect from others, especially those you respect.

Your thoughts, feelings, and emotions can be expressed.

You reserve the right to understand your own needs, share them with others, and do what you need to do to meet those needs, as long as you do not take anything away from others.

www.ingramcontent.com/pod-product-compliance
Lightning Source LLC
Chambersburg PA
CBHW071123030426
42336CB00013BA/2189